The
Connell Guide
to

———

How to write well

———

by Tim de Lisle

Cartoons by Nick Newman

"I think Connell Guides are absolutely brilliant."
William Boyd, best-selling author

Contents

Don't be afraid to dip in ...

Introduction

Writing matters. We all do it, and we all admire it when it's done well. It doesn't just express us: it represents us. It is there, on someone else's screen, when we are not there. **Writing is the second most important thing we learn at school**, after how to get along with others – and it helps with that too.

When we are seven, writing is fun, absorbing, creative, like painting or dressing up. Somewhere along the steep ascent of the next ten years, that feeling can be lost, stifled by school or smothered by self-consciousness. **This slim volume aims to bring the fun back, by showing you simple ways to write better.** It's not the last word on the subject (nothing ever is); it's a quick guide, packed with tips picked up in my life as a writer and editor.

One reason why our love of writing wilts is that it doesn't get much watering. Teachers often have their eye on something else, and perhaps (whisper it) they were never taught to write well themselves. Writing is like dancing, in that you can tell instantly if someone is good at it. But it's also like driving, in that it can be taught. If you find it hard, you're in good company: even some famous writers rely rather too heavily on their editors.

Writing is not about being a genius; few people are. It's wonderful when you see it elevated to an art, but most of the time it's just a craft. The question isn't whether you are a born writer. It's whether there is a better writer inside you, waiting to get out.

Any writing, anywhere, can be good, bad, or somewhere in between. There are tweets that are beautifully composed and trilogies that are terrible. A line jotted inside a birthday card can be just right – warm, funny or loving. A three-word slogan can be inspired, as the Conservative Party famously showed in 1979 with "Labour isn't working", or it can be drivel, as the Trainline booking service helpfully confirmed in 2016 with "i am train".

Writing will help you cope with exams, but that's not really the point. It helps you cope with life. A well-written email can land you a job; a well-written text can seal a friendship or start a romance. All you need is an open mind, a supply of energy, and the desire to improve.

Books of advice on anything are apt to be irritating, and rare is the piece of writing about good writing that doesn't end up offering examples of bad writing itself. You probably know Murphy's Law, the pessimist's charter which states that whatever can go wrong, will go wrong. Writers of books like this mutter darkly about Murphy's lesser-known twin, Muphry's law, which states that anyone who criticises someone else's writing or editing will commit some howler of their own. Your job is to see if you can spot it; mine is to apologise in advance.

You can read the book from start to finish in a couple of hours, or you can just dip in. The contents are overleaf, and there's an index at the back. I hope you find it useful, and entertaining.

1. Be clear

If you can only be one thing, be clear. It sounds like a modest ambition, but we often fall short of it. Being clear means keeping things simple, or as simple as you can without misleading the reader.

One summer, nearly a lifetime ago, a leaflet dropped on the mat of every household in Britain. It brought news of something quietly revolutionary:

> **Your new National Health Service begins on 5th July. What is it? How do you get it?**
> It will provide you with all medical, dental and nursing care. Everyone – rich or poor, man, woman or child – can use it or any part of it. There are no charges, except for a few special items. There are no insurance qualifications. But it is not a "charity". You are all paying for it, mainly as tax payers, and it will relieve your money worries in time of illness.

If medals were handed out for services to clarity, the anonymous authors of these words would have got one. They kept it magnificently simple. First, they announced the launch of an institution, in the plainest language, stating its name and giving its start date, and choosing "begin" rather than its pompous brother "commence". Then they ask two questions: "What is it? How do you get it?" All the best questions are short, because then they are big and open, leaving room for many different answers.

And this even applies, as here, with a question you ask yourself. So far we've had three sentences, but only 16 words, none of them long, which is reassuring: it says the authors have nothing to hide.

The sentences that follow, giving the answers, are almost as short as the questions. The first sentence ("It will provide...") sums up what the NHS offers, and the second spells out who can use it – everyone. The third says that nearly all of it is free; the fourth assures you that you don't need insurance. The fifth sentence and the first half of the sixth show how the service is funded. **The paragraph finishes with the emotional impact that is the point of the whole exercise – peace of mind.**

All this is done calmly, crisply, with no fuss or grandstanding. Which is not to say that it's flawless. A picky editor might quibble with "qualifications", a word of five syllables in a paragraph where everything else has three at most: it would have been plainer and simpler as "You don't need insurance". And there's another bum note in the quote marks around "charity". The point being made here is straightforward – the NHS is not a charity – so there's no need to complicate things. (Rule of thumb: save your quote marks for quoting.)

The "you" at the start of the last sentence could have been a "we". (Another rule of thumb: don't address your audience in the plural, as you're trying to connect with each one of them. Jane Eyre didn't say "Readers, I married him".) And "mainly as tax payers" could have been just "through our taxes". So the last bit might have read like this:

> ...it is not a charity: we are all paying for it through our taxes, and it will make sure that when we are ill, we don't have money worries as well.

But the original paragraph is still immensely powerful. It contains only 88 words, just under ten per sentence. It conveys all the main points about the NHS. It is direct, helpful and down-to-earth. Written in 1948, it is way ahead of its time.

Don't try to look clever

Being clear means using words the reader will understand, which means using words you understand yourself. **Being clear is way better than being clever.** If you can be both at once, all the better; but it's not worth going out of your way to sound clever. A great TV critic, Nancy Banks-Smith, said, "We cannot put pen to paper without revealing something of ourselves." When we get caught trying to look clever, we just end up looking silly.

If the temptation persists, all you have to do is look the word up. Real writers have a dictionary to hand, and they're not fussed whether it's on paper or online, as long as it's authoritative. I use Dictionary. com, launched in 1995 (before Google) and based on the Random House Unabridged Dictionary. If a word is too new for those august pages, it may well

WRITERS ON WRITING

A word after a word after a word is power.
Margaret Atwood

My task, by the power of the written word, is to make you hear, to make you feel – it is, before all, to make you see.
Joseph Conrad

True ease in writing comes from art, not chance, As those move easiest who have learn'd to dance.
Alexander Pope

Writing is the art of applying the ass to the seat.
Dorothy Parker

Substitute "damn" every time you're inclined to write "very"; your editor will delete it and the writing will be just as it should be.
Mark Twain

This letter is longer than usual, because I've not had time to make it shorter.
Blaise Pascal

If you don't have time to read, you don't have the time — or the tools — to write. Simple as that.
Stephen King

have landed at urbandictionary.com, which is just as helpful and more likely to make you laugh.

One reason the NHS blurb worked was that it had a strong sense of its reader. It could be understood by anyone who was able to read, and by many who weren't, because the short sentences made it easy to read aloud to the illiterate. The authors didn't let their phrasing get in the way of their meaning. Consciously or not, they complied with a famous maxim coined two years earlier by George Orwell: "Good prose is like a windowpane."

Orwell believed, with a passion, that the powerful need to be straight with us. He would have groaned had he lived to hear Theresa May comment on the news that she was going to be Britain's prime minister. "I'm humbled," she said, when she meant the exact opposite – I'm honoured, I'm proud. And this was someone who had presented herself as straight-talking. In the heat of the moment, she forgot that clarity breeds credibility.

Even if you're not powerful, it's vital to say what you mean (unless you're cracking a joke). Just as sportsmen talk of treating the game with respect, so anybody who writes needs to respect the language. Ambiguity can be effective – especially in a song, or a poem – but it's a weapon to add to your arsenal after getting into the habit of being clear. **First learn the rules, then think about breaking them.** Even Andy Warhol, who became world-famous for churning out big bold screenprints of photos of celebrities, had taken the trouble to learn to draw.

YOUR TURN

Being as clear and direct as you can...

a) *Invent a game and explain the rules*
   or
b) *Invent a job and apply for it*

BE PLAYFUL...

Treat this piece of advice with care: there is a time for play and it's probably not in the middle of an exam. But play is important, and it's a bigger thing than it may appear in the rear-view mirror. "Children learn through play," the pioneering musician Brian Eno said in the BBC's John Peel Lecture in 2015. "Adults play through art." And there's a lot of fun to be had in playing with words.

Take this poem by Brian Bilston, a mysterious character who has been called the Banksy of Twitter. He may be only a figment of his own imagination, but he makes thousands of people smile. While most of his poems are light entertainment, this one is playful to the point of being deadly serious.

Refugees

They have no need of our help
So do not tell me
These haggard faces could belong to you or me
Should life have dealt a different hand
We need to see them for who they really are
Chancers and scroungers
Layabouts and loungers
With bombs up their sleeves
Cut-throats and thieves
They are not
Welcome here
We should make them
Go back to where they came from
They cannot
Share our food
Share our homes
Share our countries
Instead let us
Build a wall to keep them out
It is not okay to say
These are people just like us
A place should only belong to those who are born there
Do not be so stupid to think that
The world can be looked at another way

Now read the poem from the bottom to the top. It
isn't word-perfect (the second-last line is missing an
"as"). It's not even all that poetic. But it makes one
point so strongly that it stays with you. Last time I
looked, it had been re-tweeted 12,000 times.

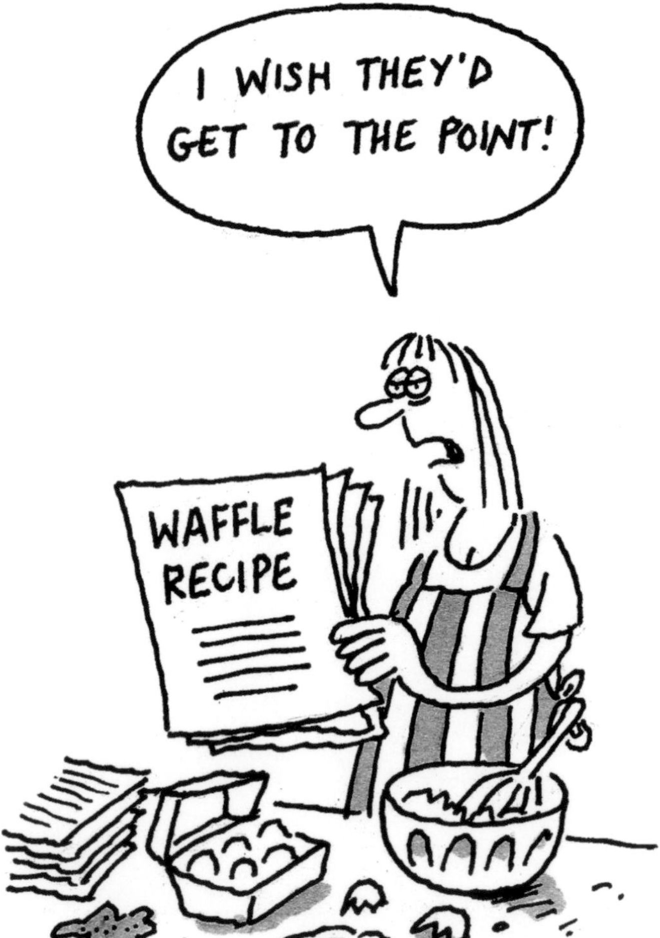
I WISH THEY'D GET TO THE POINT!
WAFFLE RECIPE

2. Be concise

Brevity, Polonius says in *Hamlet*, is the soul of wit. It's a great line, coolly practising what it preaches (while also poking fun at Polonius himself, for banging on). You could take it further and say that **brevity is the soul of writing.** The words we write bite into our readers' time, so it is good manners not to be greedy. Waffle, while delicious for breakfast, is tiresome on the page, and readers, especially teachers and examiners, can spot it a mile off.

Every so often, someone somewhere launches a short-story competition in which the story has to be only six words long. The most famous example is thought to have been written by Ernest Hemingway:

For sale, baby shoes, never worn.

Whoever it's by, it could hardly be better. It has a twist, and uses it to do something Gustave Flaubert said writers longed for – **to move the stars to pity**.

Don't pad out your sentence

Twitter is sometimes dismissed as dumbed-down because of its 140-character limit. Yet that story would have fitted into a tweet, no trouble. Twitter forces us to do something we should be doing anyway as we write: to distil our thoughts. Sometimes this is just a matter of finding the right word, and not using four or five where one will do. If you're tempted to write "despite the fact that", bear in mind that we already have a word for it: "although". "Increase the size of": try "increase" on its own, or one of its sisters – "enlarge" or "expand". "At this moment in time": how about "now"?

In language, as in decorating a room, **there are some frills that are not worth having.** "Amongst" adds nothing to "among" bar a whiff of pretension, and the same goes for "whilst" and "while". The extra letters sit there like a doily on the table, making you look, by modern standards, mildly ridiculous.

That said, it's possible to take compression too far. Writing can become too staccato if it's just one short sentence after another. Advice, especially, can be too bald: "do not be hectoring or arrogant," says *The Economist Style Guide*, making a valid point in a way which, as one reviewer pointed out, is quite hectoring and arrogant itself. And there are few characters in life more maddening than the friend whose texts are relentlessly terse.

It helps to start and finish any personal communication with a thought about the other person ("hope you're well", "love you"). If you get into a rapid exchange of views, this rule is suspended in the middle. It's like playing tennis: you need to be sure your opponent is ready for a serve, but you don't need to worry once the rally is under way.

Two kinds of padding are particularly worth watching out for. One is saying the same thing twice; in an effort not to do it myself, I'll say more about this in Chapter 6. The other is self-consciousness. Self-awareness is a strength, self-consciousness a pain, and it's all too easy to tip over from one to the other. One easy way to avoid it is this: **don't mention yourself unless you have to.** If you've written "I think", try deleting it: by being less self-conscious, your opinion will instantly carry more weight.

Just beyond self-consciousness, two more dangers lie in wait for us – self-obsession and self-delusion. Among his other gifts to writers, Donald Trump is a warning to us all on this front.

"I think I'm actually humble," Trump told a TV interviewer in July 2016. "I think I'm much more humble than you would understand." If he was really humble, (a) he wouldn't say so, (b) he wouldn't presume that the interviewer wouldn't understand, and (c) he wouldn't keep using "I".

Just say it

On the whole, it's better just to say things than to say things about the things you are saying. Even a phrase like "Put simply" can rub people up the wrong way: putting things simply is great, as we've seen, but commenting on your ability to do so may have the reader groaning and muttering "get on with it". Phrases like "It would be no exaggeration to say that" contain more than their share of hot air. As Oscar Wilde almost said, it's the importance of being not too earnest.

YOUR TURN

1. Write your own very short story – in six words if you can, but feel free to stretch to 12. If you're on Twitter, or know someone who is, send it to me @TimdeLisle.

2. Here's a tweet posted by a bestselling novelist in June 2016, just before the EU referendum. He packs six predictions and a question into 140 characters.

Robert Harris *@Robert_Harris*
Scenario: Leave win. PM resigns. Boris leader. No majority for Brexit in Commons. Autumn election to seek mandate. Tories split. Then what?

Write your own tweet, making at least three predictions in no more than 140 characters. They don't have to be right: by the end of April, only half of Harris's six had come true.

WHY WRITE?

At times, as you plod through another essay or email, you may wonder what writing is for. It's a question that might elicit a hundred different answers. Mine goes like this.

We write **to connect with other people** – to make them laugh, or cry, or think.

We also write **to work out what we think ourselves**: there's nothing like it for concentrating the mind. Don DeLillo writes big fat novels and looks as if he's got it all worked out, but he once said: "I don't know what I think about certain subjects, even today, until I sit down and try to write about them." That's a nice "try".

We write **to tell a story, to capture a truth, to persuade, or to entertain**. It could be an email or an essay, a letter, a job application, or the dreaded personal statement for university. Writing isn't just writing, it's doing. It can show gratitude, cement a relationship, boost our chances of getting on in life.

We write **to express ourselves.** A couple of years ago I reported on the charity First Story, which sets up after-school writing groups led by authors (general idea: have a biscuit, write a poem). The students' self-esteem rose as they displayed a talent they hadn't known they possessed. And it's not just self-esteem. Our writing represents us when we're not there; it can give a good impression of us or a bad one. Not all these lights are switched on all the time, but they never go out all at once.

GOOD TO SEE THE IMPROVEMENT IN SPELLING AND PUNCTUATION
ST JUDE'S ACADEMY
DOWN WITH SCHOOL!
TEACHERS SMELL
THE HEAD' S A MUPPET!

3. Be vivid

At the risk of stating the obvious, **writing is an activity.** George Mackay Brown, probably the most famous author to come from Orkney, used to say that a writer was like a farmer or a carpenter. It may not look this way to anyone wandering past as you sit there and stare at your screen, but you are making something. You need to bring energy to the task. Dip into Caitlin Moran (in The Times Magazine every Saturday, in the bookshops all the time) and see how much she puts into every paragraph.

You won't write well if you're distracted or dopey: **the writing gods expect you to be switched on.** This doesn't mean resorting to cups of coffee or cans of Red Bull – just making sure you're concentrating, if only for half an hour. Treat it as a series of sprints, and you should soon find yourself in the 800 metres. But you may need to tune out of social media first.

If you're switched on, your sentences are likely to be the third thing they most need to be, after clear and concise: vivid. Bad writing lands dead on the page, whereas good writing is alive. And what gives it life, more often than not, is that it is visual.

A picture may be worth a thousand words, but **a thousand words can be a gallery of pictures.** There's no literary mantra more vital than "show and tell", and it's not an accident that "show" comes first. Good writers give examples, catch our eye and tickle our ear, take something mundane or middling and make it memorable.

Many of us have noticed that bad things seem to happen in clusters, but only Shakespeare, writing *Hamlet* circa 1600, put it like this: "When sorrows come, they come not single spies/But in battalions." And only Neil Gaiman, in his novel *Neverwhere* (1996), put it like this: "Richard had noticed that events were cowards: they didn't occur singly, but instead they would run in packs and leap out at him all at once." The observation may be an obvious one, but Shakespeare and Gaiman transform it by adding vividness. Like a friend visiting a family and turning up with a present for the children, they bring something eye-catching: the spies and the cowards.

Ever since team games took off and nation started playing against nation, the thought has occurred to people that sport has a certain amount in common with war. But it took George Orwell to crystallise it: "Sport is war minus the shooting."

Many people have sat around in a group and seen it come to the wrong decision, but only one of them, long since lost in the mists of time, put it like this: "A camel is a horse designed by a committee." There's a school of thought that this was cruel to camels, just as the ex-ghostwriter who said of Donald Trump, "I put lipstick on a pig", should surely have received a lawsuit from the sty. But writing doesn't have a duty to be inarguably right. It has a duty to encapsulate things, and the pig and the camel make that happen.

One of the best-loved novels of the 21st century, *Wolf Hall* (2009), retells the tale of Henry VIII through the eyes of his chief minister, Thomas

Cromwell. Hilary Mantel could have begun with Cromwell's first day working for Henry, or his first brush with Anne Boleyn, but instead she starts years earlier, with Cromwell as a teenager, in Putney, being beaten up, by his own father. Or rather lying in the gutter, straight afterwards. "I heard a voice saying 'Now get up'," she told 700 people at the Union Chapel in Islington in 2014.

It was the voice of Cromwell's father, reeking of contempt, untroubled by remorse, let alone love.

THE DOS AND DON'TS OF DON'T AND WON'T

Don't, won't and *can't, he's* and *she's* and *they're* are all fine – they save a syllable, they get us to the point quicker, they feel natural and they've long since become part of the furniture. If someone disapproves of them, you could gently ask whether they disapprove of "goodbye" too, on the grounds that it started life as "God be with you". That said, contractions shouldn't be compulsory. There are times when we can do with the extra muscle of the separate words ("Do not pass Go", "You cannot be serious"). And it can be effective to mix the two modes: "It is well known that a vital ingredient of success is not knowing that what you're attempting can't be done" (Terry Pratchett, *Equal Rites*, 1987). The only contractions to steer clear of are *would've, could've* and *should've*: they look clunky and save no syllables, because they sound just the same as the words they're trying to replace. Still, at least they're not *would of*.

"And then all the decisions about the novel had been made." It can't have been that easy, but it makes a good story. And it's striking that Mantel opens with the incident that gives her Cromwell his motivation.

Something else she said that night sticks in the memory. "People suppose that imagination is an airy quality, and that employing it is a genteel act that might be done on a chaise longue. But to imagine properly, you have to imagine strenuously. It involves your whole body, from feet to head." So creative writing is closer to acting than we might think. Mantel was sharing the stage with an eminent actress, Harriet Walter, and even in saying this, she was putting her arguments into pictures – the whole body, the head, the feet, and, best of all, with its air of useless affluence, the chaise longue.

Sometimes you need to do the telling before the showing, to set up your best line. In *The History Boys* (2006), a wonderful play but one that is almost as male as its name suggests, Alan Bennett has a character called Mrs Lintott, a teacher who is the voice of reason, scepticism and feminism. "History," she proclaims, "is a commentary on the various and continuing incapabilities of men."

By Bennett's high standards, this is rather a dry sentence, all abstract nouns and no pictures. But we soon discover that it's only the set-up.

"What is history?" Mrs Lintott goes on. "History is women following behind with the bucket."

SURPRISING THE READER

In *Such, Such were the Joys* (1952), George Orwell writes about something he felt as a small boy:

> Love, the spontaneous, unqualified emotion of love, was something I could only feel for people who were young. Towards people who were old ... I could feel reverence, respect, admiration or compunction, but I seemed cut off from them by a veil of fear and shyness mixed up with physical distaste. People are too ready to forget the child's physical shrinking from the adult. The enormous size of grown-ups, their ungainly, rigid bodies, their coarse wrinkled skins, their great relaxed eyelids, their yellow teeth, and the whiffs of musty clothes and beer and sweat and tobacco that disengage from them at every movement!

Orwell believed that writing should be clear and vigorous, and this passage is both. In *Strictly English* (2010) Simon Heffer salutes its "astonishing clarity"; on some things, Heffer and I have to agree to differ, but not here. Orwell has worked out what he wants to say and says it with passion and precision, showing us some things ("cut off by a veil") and telling us others ("fear and shyness ... physical distaste"). He uses his senses, capturing smells and sights: the grown-ups have "rigid bodies", "coarse wrinkled skins", four different whiffs, and, best of all, "great relaxed eyelids". Being relaxed is usually a happy state, and "great", too, tends to be a good thing, but Orwell remembers how big and droopy those eyelids seemed to him, and finds words to say so that turn two pluses into a minus – in a good way.

YOUR TURN

1. When sorrows come, they come not in single spies/ But in battalions. – **Shakespeare**

Think of another vivid way to show that troubles seem to turn up in clusters.

2. Don't tell me the moon is shining; show me the glint of light on broken glass. – **Anton Chekhov**

Find a vivid way to end these two sentences:

(a) Don't tell me it's raining; show me

(b) Don't tell me you went on holiday; show me

3. Read this passage from Charlie and the Chocolate Factory (1964) by Roald Dahl:

> Charlie Bucket stared around the gigantic room in which he now found himself. The place was like a witch's kitchen! All about him black metal pots were boiling and bubbling on huge stoves, and kettles were hissing and pans were sizzling, and strange iron machines were clanking and spluttering, and there were pipes running all over the ceiling and walls, and the whole place was filled with smoke and steam and delicious rich smells.

Then think of a room, real or imagined, and try to have as much fun describing it as Dahl did there.

NOT A HIP WAS WRIGGLED...

The book that did most to inspire this one is *Put It in Writing* (1984) by John Whale, a guide so crisp and wise that every intern I ever hired ended up reading it. Early on, Whale champions this passage from *Pax Britannica* (1968) by James Morris (now Jan Morris), showing what Sundays were like in a border town in Canada in the 1890s.

> The bars, theatres and dance halls closed at a minute before midnight every Saturday night, and not a whisky was sold again, not a hip was wriggled, not a bet was placed, until two in the morning on Monday. The Sunday sounds of Dawson City were psalms and snores. No kind of work was allowed. Men were arrested for fishing on a Sunday, or for sawing wood. The only hope of living it up, between Saturday night and Monday morning, was to take a boat downriver and slip across the line into the States – out of reach of the Pax Britannica and its stern schoolmarm values.

A less sparky writer might have said something like this. "Sundays in Dawson City were sacrosanct, reserved for going to church or going to sleep. The residents were not allowed to dance, gamble, buy alcohol, go fishing or even do any work, unless they crossed the border into the United States, out of reach of the British Empire and its Victorian values."

That would have summed up the situation solidly enough and saved 60 words or so, but it would have deprived us of the whisky, the hip, the wriggle, the bet, the psalms, the snores, the fishing, the sawing and the boat, not to mention the bars, the theatres, the dance halls and the precise timings. It would have drained the colour from the passage, and much of the life: there would have been hardly anything to see or hear or smell or feel – let alone remember.

Morris's paragraph isn't difficult or demanding. The pace is quick, the words are short, the tone is informal, and yet there's some shape. All those sights and sounds are there to work up to the main point, which uses the title of the book and punches it home with one well-chosen word – "schoolmarm". It's like watching a string of passes, wondering where they're going, and then seeing the ball in the back of the net. To write well, John Whale says, "you should think in pictures, write as you speak, and keep your reader happy". This passage does all of that.

Be conversational

It will make your writing intelligible, digestible, enjoyable. You'll have to be selective too – pure conversation, with its *um*s and *er*s and *like*s, doesn't work on the page, except (obviously) as dialogue. But it's easy to go too far the other way. **Fine writing has less to do with formality than you might think.** Homer, the first great writer in the Western world, was an epic poet, yet he was described by Matthew Arnold, a Victorian professor of poetry, as "eminently rapid ... eminently plain and direct".

Hamilton (2015) by Lin-Manuel Miranda, already one of the great Broadway hits, is deliciously conversational. It's a history play about one of America's founding fathers, written in a way that is boldly contemporary. "We hold these truths to be self-evident that all men are created equal," sings one of the characters, Angelica, in a song called The Schuyler Sisters. Miranda deserves a medal just for fitting that line to music, but he has more. "When I meet Thomas Jefferson," Angelica goes on, "I'm-a compel him to include women in the sequel." Coming straight after Jefferson, that "I'm-a" captures the collisions – between past and present, white and black, rigidity and diversity – that the show is all about.

Switching from talking to writing is like getting ready for a night out. You're not putting on fancy dress, or trying to look like someone else; you're going as yourself, but making more effort, being a bit smarter, getting closer to your best.

Give your vocab an upgrade

We all have our pet words, and the reader may soon tire of them. Whole societies have their favourites too. In the English language in the 21st century, "literally" and "genuinely" have joined the club of words that act as a sort of social glue. But they won't do much for your writing. "Literally", in written English, leans back towards its original meaning – "not figuratively" – so it works with that hat on, but not as an all-purpose form of emphasis. "Genuinely" works if the context has led us to think something might not be genuine, but, again, not as a mere prop. One way to test a word like "genuinely" is by writing your sentence with it in place, then taking it out, and seeing if the sentence works better. It usually will, because "genuinely", like "to be honest", can easily backfire, saying more about your credibility than about your subject.

REPETITION OR VARIATION?

One of the redeeming features of illness is that you can't infect yourself – that nasty cold of yours can't give you another cold. One of the tricky things about writing is that you can infect yourself. We're inclined to use a word or phrase or construction, then use it again five minutes later – and what was five minutes for us may be only five seconds for the reader.

Repetition isn't always bad: there are some famous lines that run on it. "To be or not to be." "The name's Bond – James Bond." "Never apologise, never explain" (horrible advice, handsomely expressed). Repetition is powerful, but perilous – it can easily bore or bug the reader, it can be distracting or jarring, especially if it's accidental, and we can usually tell. But sometimes variation is worse, especially if it means dumbly replacing a name with a description. You're reading a news story about Adele and she suddenly becomes "the 28-year-old", "the millionaire singer" and then "the *Skyfall* star", none of which feels natural, and one of which is surely Daniel Craig. The best option may well be the simplest one, "she" or "her", which will probably mean rejigging the sentence. Repetition is often a side-effect of structure.

Sometimes the problem lies not with the second use of a word, but the first. "J.L. Carr's masterpiece *A Month in the Country* only runs to 85 pages," said Standpoint magazine in May 2016. "If only more writers realised that length isn't everything." It's a shrewd point, crisply phrased, apart from that repeat of "only", which is a clodhopper. The second "only" is needed, because "if only" is an idiom meaning "I wish that", but the first "only" isn't, and it's easily replaced: you could say *A Month in the Country* runs to just 85 pages" or "runs to a mere 85 pages". There are about 180,000 English words in current use, according to the Oxford English Dictionary, and you can often get yourself out of a tight corner by reaching for a fresh one.

YOUR TURN

Here is a clumsy sentence quoted in The Penguin Writer's Manual *(2002).*

> *One of the most attractive things about South Africa is the fact that it has such a variety of different scenery.*

Try reading it aloud. As the authors of the manual say, it has a "kind of stutter" in the middle, because of all the short words in a row. Can you rewrite it to make it run more smoothly? (See foot of page 34)

4. Know the basics

Tennis players have to know the difference between a serve and a volley, and practise both – even if they're among the best in the world. Writing is much the same. The fundamental things apply, and you need a firm grasp of them. Looking at other books on writing, I found that they were apt to get bogged down in the finer points of grammar, so this book is just going to give you the basics. They are rough and ready, and leave out some of the many exceptions to the rules, but they will stand you in good stead 95 times out of 100.

Answer: Your Turn (page 33)

There's more than one way to fix this, but the simplest is to cut the words in the middle – as well as "different", which adds nothing to "variety".

One of the most attractive things about South Africa is the variety of its scenery.

All the grammar you need

Remember your teacher long ago talking about the parts of speech? If you didn't take it in then, now is the time to nail it. For the full story, you need a grammar book (the most entertaining is *For Who The Bell Tolls* by David Marsh, 2013 – and yes, the "who" is deliberate). This is a rough guide, designed to get you through most situations. "Part of speech" can be an off-putting phrase, but it just means a group of words that do much the same job.

Parts of speech

There are four big ones...

a noun	a thing – one you can see or touch (*chair, bus, cake*) or one you can't (*peace, love, understanding*). The ones you can't see or touch are abstract nouns. The ones with capital letters (*Paris, Facebook, Beyoncé*) are proper nouns
a verb	a doing word *go, see, live, love, laugh*
an adjective	a word that describes a noun – *good, bad, hot, cold, supercalifragilistic-expialidocious*
an adverb	the same, but for verbs – *well, badly, hotly, coldly*

... Four little ones ...

a pronoun	a little word that saves us having to use names all the time – *I, you, he, she, it, we, they*
a preposition	a little word that tells you where things are – *in, on, up, down, to, from*. Or modifies the meaning of a verb: *to piss* is not the same thing as to *piss off*
a conjunction	a little or medium-sized word that joins two thoughts – *and, but, if, though*
an exclamation	a little word that expresses a greeting or response, like an emoticon – *yes, no, wow, hey, OMG, d'oh*, and many swearwords

... And a few minor ones

a number	you've known what they are since you were about *three*
an article	a little word that goes before a noun – *the, a, an*. Some languages don't bother with them
a determiner	a little word that distinguishes one thing from another – *this, that, either, both*
a gerund	a noun made out of a verb – *seeing* is *believing*. Latin gerunds end in – *ndum*, and some live on as English words: *memorandum, addendum*, and the fateful *referendum*

Tenses

The three basic ones...

the present	*I love you.*
the past	*I loved you once.*
the future	*I will always love you.*

The three continuous ones...

the continuous present	something happening now, but not only at this moment: *I am studying Arabic.* In questions, we use it a lot: *What are you doing?*
the present perfect	something that began in the past and hasn't stopped: *I've loved you for a long, long time.*
the imperfect	something in the past that carried on for a while: *When the earthquake began, I was eating my lunch.*

... And the two uncommon ones

| the pluperfect | needed when you're already in the past and want to go back further: *She had loved him once.* |
| the future perfect | needed when you're in the future and want to go back a bit: *By 2020, they will have been together for 30 years.* |

Verbs have moods too. Six main ones...

The indicative   the one you don't have to think about, because most verbs are in it, including both the verbs in this sentence. It's "the mood ... used for ordinary objective statements, questions, etc" (Dictionary.com)

The imperative   telling someone to do something: *Go – walk out the door.*

The subjunctive   showing "what is imagined or wished or possible" (Oxford Dictionaries.com). Can be hard to spot. As Ralph Fiennes says, over and over again, in *Hail Caesar!* (2016): *Would that it were so simple.*

The conditional   may or might, mainly: *You may come too; I might even enjoy it.*

The infinitive   the purest form of the verb, with "to" in front of it, to denote its essence: *To err is human, to forgive divine.*

The interrogative   for questions: *Do you love him?* It goes last here, partly because it may not count as a separate mood, and partly to make sure that this quick guide has gone to the infinitive and beyond.

Punctuation on a plate

The bread and butter ...

Full stop

a pause between sentences: *The cat sat on the mat. Then it saw a mouse.*

Comma

a shorter pause in mid-sentence: *The cat sat on the mat, until it saw a mouse.*

In pairs, a way to park a description or a name: *The cat, which was fast becoming an internet sensation, sat on the mat.*

The England manager, Gareth Southgate, has named his first squad.

Apostrophe

(i) to show that a final S is possessive, not plural: *I love Bart's hair in* The Simpsons.

(ii) to stand in for the missing letter in a contraction: *don't, won't, wasn't, it's* (which is always short for *it is* or *it has*)

Hyphen

to show that two words are parcelled up as one part of speech: *the full-time whistle (because* it's not a full whistle, or a time whistle). Also needed when a noun and a preposition team up to form a noun:

	I left my passport at check-in – but not when the same two words team up to form a verb: *You need a passport to check in.*
Question mark	to show you're asking a question. *Got it?*
Exclamation mark	to show you're exclaiming. *Got it!* (Best not used for jokes, or in large numbers. "Five exclamation marks," Terry Pratchett said, "the sure sign of an insane mind")
Quote marks	to show the words are someone else's, or yours in the past. *"You're fired," said Lord Sugar. "You're joking," I replied.*

... And the jam

Colon	to show that one point leads on to the next. *The past is a foreign country: they do things differently there.* Or to introduce a list. *England squad: Cook, Hameed, Root...*
Semi-colon	to show that two points exist in parallel. *Some people specialise; others juggle.* Or to separate items on a list, when some of them include a comma: *Also on the bill are Damon Albarn, with the Orchestra of Syrian*

	Musicians; the Last Shadow Puppets, featuring Alex Turner from the Arctic Monkeys; and the Labour leader, Jeremy Corbyn.
Dash	on its own, for when the train of thought takes a sudden turn. *The cat sat on the mat – the mouse mat.* in pairs: a way of parking one thought inside another. *The cat – true to form – sat on the mat.*
Brackets	to show that your point is an aside. (Brackets are always found in pairs. If a sentence begins inside them, it ends inside them too.)
Ellipsis	three dots, showing that you've left some words out of a quote, or that your point is knowingly unfinished, or you want it to hover in the air...

Quote marks are for quoting

Nervous writers tend to overdo the quote marks, as if unaware that there's a good way of using them and a bad way. The good way is, as the name suggests, for quoting. If you use somebody's exact words, quote marks are needed, as a graceful acknowledgement (these words aren't mine) that can also be a useful get-out (I didn't say this, Donald Trump did).

The bad way is when you're not quoting anyone, just trying to handle a word with rubber gloves. "The great sweep of economic history," Bloomberg Businessweek argued after the Brexit vote, "is a series of 'rises' and 'falls' — from the fall of Rome to the rise of China." The second rise, and the second fall, are the right ones – no quote marks required.

If in doubt

Keep it simple. Full stops are your friend, and so are commas. Colons and semi-colons are good cards to play as long as you know the difference between them. If not, they leave you trying hard to appear clever, which is never a good look (see chapter 1). And even when you get them right, they are best used sparingly – if one sentence has a colon or semi-colon, let the next one flow.

Commas between adjectives

When using two or three adjectives together, most people separate them with a comma or a conjunction. "The stranger was tall, dark and handsome." If you favour a second comma there, after "dark", you're a believer in the Oxford comma, which is fine as long as you're consistent about it.

Sometimes you can just run one adjective after the other to quicken the pace. "It was a bright cold day in April," Orwell begins *Nineteen Eighty Four* (1948), "and the clocks were striking thirteen."

Philip Pullman takes this a step further and turns it into a party trick. "She laid it on the table," he writes of Lyra in *Northern Lights* (1995), "and she sensed John Faa's massive simple curiosity and

Farder Coram's bright flickering intelligence both trained on it like searchlights."

Comma of the century, so far

If there was an award for the best piece of punctuation – and there surely should be – the mantelpiece at Lin-Manuel Miranda's place in New York would be even more congested than it already is. Of all the bright ideas in his masterpiece, *Hamilton* (2015), the deftest may be the comma that occurs when the main character is writing to his wife's sister. "My dearest, Angelica," he begins. She doesn't return the comma ("My dearest Alexander"), but she does pick him up on it:

> In a letter I received from you two weeks ago I
> noticed a comma in the middle of a phrase.
> It changed the meaning. Did you intend this?
> One stroke and you've consumed my waking days.

Hamilton doesn't answer, except to acknowledge the comma's presence. He doesn't have to, as we sense that it wouldn't be there if it wasn't loaded with meaning. On Twitter, Lin-Manuel Miranda confirms as much: "That sh*t took weeks."

Syntax without tears

Clauses

A clause is a group of words that contains a subject and a verb. The cat doesn't have to sit on the mat to make a clause – it just has to do something. "The cat yawned": that's enough.

Clauses are like people on motorbikes: they're either in the driving seat or the sidecar – they're either a main clause or a subordinate clause. "The cat yawned" is a main clause. "When the cat yawned" is a subordinate clause. It needs a main clause with it to make a complete sentence: "When the cat yawned, the dog barked."

Relative clauses – the ones that begin with "who" or "which" or "whom" or "whose" or occasionally "that", and are not questions – are always subordinate. "The cat, which had got the cream, sat on the mat."

Phrases

A phrase is a small group of words that come together to form a unit but not a clause. "On the mat" is a phrase. "The cat sat" is not, because it contains a main verb.

Word order

A lot of the time it's straightforward – just follow your instinct. "The cat has got the cream." Nobody would put those words in any other order, unless they were Yoda, or a particularly desperate songwriter.

English has no trouble with the basic trio of subject-verb-object, but when they are joined by an adverb, things get complicated.

I will be with you, whatever. But this is the moment to assess bluntly the difficulties.

Tony Blair, memo to George W. Bush, 2002, disclosed in the Chilcot Report, July 2016

The first of these sentences has already gone down in history as a blank cheque for which hundreds of thousands of people paid with their lives. But it's the second, the more sensible of the two, that gets into a tangle. Blair put "bluntly" in an odd place, probably because he was straining to avoid a split infinitive ("to bluntly assess"). The best way out might have been to stick with the same words and tweak the syntax: "But this is the moment to be blunt in assessing the difficulties."

Front-loading

Many an excellent sentence has a bit that comes before the subject. But so do some bad ones – because the writer forgets that the bit at the front applies to the whole sentence.

In 2005 she founded a karaoke club business, two years later joined the board of Marks & Spencer, and has just become a non-executive director of Twitter.

The Times on Martha Lane Fox, May 2016

"In 2005" applies to the whole shebang, so it contradicts "two years later" and "has just". It's a problem that is easily fixed: you just need another "she" after "two years later", and a third before "has just". This is one of those moments when repetition is the lesser of the evils.

Rules worth obeying

Don't split the infinitive

Of all the bees in the stickler's bonnet, this may be the one with the loudest buzz. For some reason, perhaps because the infinitive has a certain purity to it, the idea arose long ago that you shouldn't park an adverb, or anything else, just after the "to".

There are ways round it. You can rephrase, as with the Tony Blair quote on page 44, or see if the adverb can be cut. The Football Association has a mission statement which includes the line: "England teams aim to intelligently dominate possession selecting the right moments to progress the play and penetrate the opposition." As sentences go, this is like England's performance against Iceland in 2016, so bad you hardly know where to begin. But one phrase stands out like a missed penalty – "to intelligently dominate". It's weird (because in sport, any old domination will do), it's clearly written by a committee, and it's a split infinitive. Next time that committee meets, its members need to ditch the claim to intelligence, or detach it from their dreams of domination.

Do bother with "whom"

"Those whom the gods love die young," the saying goes. It seems that the gods are not great fans of "whom", which has lived to a great age and has been dying a slow and painful death for decades. To the traditionalist, "whom" is needed whenever the relative pronoun is not the subject of the verb, so you have "Romeo, who loves Juliet", or "Romeo, whom Juliet loves". To the modernist, "whom" feels stiff and starchy, and isn't needed, because the word order tells us who is loving who(m). The traditionalist retorts that we still use "him", which is another example of a Saxon accusative, as are "her", "me", "us" and "them". The modernist notes that "you" doesn't have an accusative and we don't miss it. The person who can see both sides stifles a yawn and wonders if we can move on.

My feeling is that it is still, just, worth bothering with "whom", as long as you can use it with confidence. If not, you may need to mug up on the difference between subjects and objects.

The simple rule: rejig the sentence, replacing "who" or "whom" with the third-person pronoun. If you find it should be "he", "she" or "they", then "who" is right; if it's "him", "her" or "them", then "whom" is right. (And if it's "it", it won't help you, as "it" is "it" whether it's the subject or the object.)

If you're still not confident after that, stick with "who" for the moment. This is what Wayne Rooney does. "Sir Alex [Ferguson] was really clever like that," he told the Daily Mail in 2016. "He knew who

he could have a go at, who it was best to leave alone."
To the stickler, each "who" should be a "whom". To
most people, it's a perfectly decent sentence, clear
and informative. Even if Rooney had written it in an
exam, he wouldn't have been marked down.

Rules worth breaking

Don't start a sentence with And or But

This is just nonsense. The King James Bible, one of
the most stylish books ever written, starts thousands
of sentences with "And". You can begin a title with
it: "And I Love Her" is one of the Beatles' best-loved
album tracks. And it can even be the first word of a
whole piece. William Blake's poem Jerusalem, now
best known as a majestic hymn, begins: "And did
those feet in ancient time ..."

Don't end a sentence with a preposition

> She looked at me closely; she was nice to be looked
> at by.   **Julian Barnes, Metroland (1980)**

That line hits the spot because it feels new and rings
true. It ends with not one preposition but two.
Barnes is a precise stylist who, not long before he
wrote that, had been working as a lexicographer on
the Oxford English Dictionary. (He had the rare
honour of writing the entry on "fuck".) He would
have known he was breaking a rule, and he was right
to, because it's an odd rule, more a matter of taste

than anything else, and poorly suited to English, with its abundance of verbs that end in a preposition – just look at "look at", "look out", "look into", "look over", "look up" and "look back".

The rule was famously mocked by Winston Churchill, rounding on an editor who cited it: "This is arrant pedantry, up with which I will not put." The story may be apocryphal, but the point is valid – all the more so as time goes on, and writing, inch by inch, becomes less formal.

Not all mistakes are equal

Mistakes sit on a sliding scale. The worst are the ones that change your meaning. The next worst are the ones that make it ambiguous. Then come the ones that make you look stupid, which include some of the most common mis-spellings. Fourth come the tiny typos that just make you look a little careless:

> **Uni of Leicester** @uniofleicester 5h
> A top 1% world university & Britian's most affordable university. Study with us this September. Open Day 22 July.

And last come the changes made by your auto-correct, which also make you look careless, but at least come with half an excuse. Auto-correct can be maddening, but it wouldn't have let "Britian" into that tweet.

We need to talk about ... tautology

Tautology is when you make the same point twice in the same sentence.

Costs can't be cheap or expensive. They can only be high or low; it's the thing you're buying that is cheap or expensive.

You can forward an email, or pass it on, but you can't forward it on; you can watch, or look on, but you can't watch on.

Things can't revert back to how they were. The "re-" in revert means back, so "revert back" doesn't add anything, except the suspicion that you don't know what you're talking about

---

YOUR TURN

Lose the unnecessary word in each of these lines.

They'll be stranded alone for a month.
Bear Grylls, Channel 4

We mustn't over-exaggerate.
Tim Henman, BBC 5 Live

United Together
Banner, Democrat National Congress

Answers on page 56

Easy mistakes to make

Often misspelt

Embarrassment it has to have that double R before the ass

Harassment single R – it rhymes with embarrassment, but doesn't share the double R

Separate not seperate because it's derived from paro in Latin – to prepare or get

Accommodation needs the double M as well as the double C

Independent three Es, no A; same with independence

Descendants two Es, one A

Surprise needs an R either side of the P (because it comes from French: sur + prise)

Liaise needs an I either side of the A

Beginning needs a double N

Often mistaken for each other

You're and your   "You're" is short for you are; "your" isn't short for anything – it means "belonging to you".

Its and it's   "Its" always, but always, means "of it"; "it's" never means "of it" – it's short for "it is" or "it has".

They're, their and there   "They're" is always short for "they are"; "their" always means "belonging to them"; "there" means "in that place". Only "there" goes with "is".

Whose and who's   "Whose" always means "of whom"; "who's" is always short for "who is" or "who has".

Effect and affect   To effect is to make something happen: *he effected his getaway.* To affect is to influence, or put on: *the red card affected the result; she affected an accent.*

Differ and defer   To differ is to be different or to disagree; to defer is to put off.

Cease and seize   To cease is to stop or desist; to seize is to grab or confiscate.

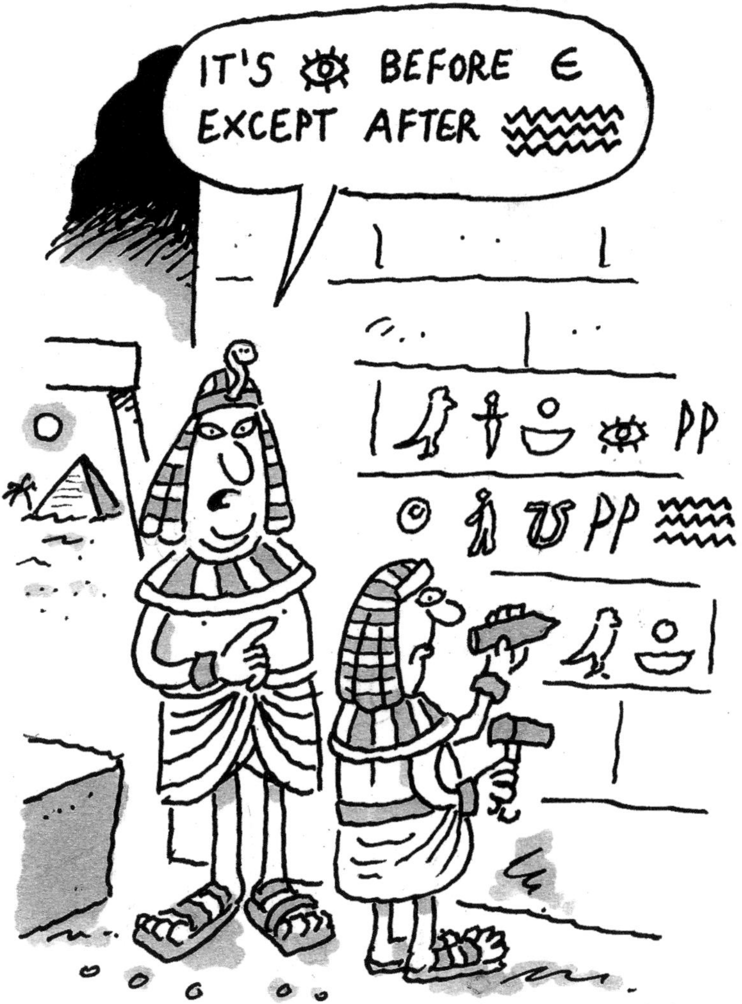
IT'S BEFORE ∈
EXCEPT AFTER

Flu, flew and flue Flu, short for influenza, is a bug; flew is the past tense of fly; a flue is a duct for smoke.

Imply and infer To imply something is to hint at it; to infer is to take the hint.

Led and lead Led is always the past tense of lead (which rhymes with weed); lead (which rhymes with wed) is never the past tense of lead, because it's a metal.

Lent and leant Lent is the past tense of lend; leant is the past tense of lean.

Past and passed The past is the time that has been and gone, and past is also a preposition meaning after: *it's past your bedtime.* Passed is always the past tense of pass: *she passed her test.*

Lose and loose Loose is the opposite of tight; lose is the opposite of gain, win or find.

Choice or option You can have many options, but you can't have many choices – a choice is between two or more options.

Refute and deny "Deny" means refuse to admit the truth of something. "Refute" means give evidence to disprove something.

That and which "That" defines; "which" informs. "I'm going to cook the mushrooms that I picked in the wood" means I will only cook those mushrooms. "I'm going to cook the mushrooms, which I picked in the wood" means I'm going to cook all my mushrooms.

Often misused

Anticipate doesn't mean "expect" – at least not according to the purists, who insist that it means "pre-empt".

Reticent doesn't mean "reluctant".

Constantly doesn't mean "repeatedly": that's "continually"

Nor means "and ... not", so can't have "and" in front of it

What goes with what

Prevent takes from *You've got to prevent them from doing that.*

Stop doesn't take from *You've got to stop them doing that.*

Different takes from *She's different from you – she loves the sound of German.* You wouldn't say "This one differs to that one".

Reticent doesn't take a verb That's reluctant, meaning not keen – "reluctant to speak out"

Congratulate takes on *I congratulate you on your excellent grammar.*

Half of writing is editing

And you've come along at the right time for it, because your screen makes crossing out easier than it has ever been. It's trying to tell you something.

Answers: Your Turn (page 50)

alone, over, together

Be consistent

Writing is like parenting: often, it's not the choice you make that matters most, but whether you stick to it. If you start a story in the present tense, stay in it unless the story demands that you switch. If you prefer to spell judgement as judgment, that's fine by the dictionary, but you need to keep on doing it. If you use double quote marks, don't switch to single, except for a quote within a quote.

If you refer to Richard III, you can call him Richard at the next mention, but you can't call him Gloucester, or Richard, Duke of Gloucester, without making it clear that this is the same person at an earlier stage. If you use "you" meaning "one", don't change to "one" in mid-stream. Better still, don't use that kind of "one" at all: leave it to the royal family.

The place where consistency counts the most is the singular and the plural. "Whoop whoop" is not the same as "whoops"; your wit is your ability to be funny, but your wits are your brain as a whole. And this is about more than a misplaced S. It's often about remembering the subject of your sentence.

"Manchester police baffled," says the Manchester Evening News, "after reports of a dead animal in the canal turns out to be a duvet filled with coconuts".

It sounds a cracking story, but it would be even better if the plural subject of the subordinate clause, "reports of a dead animal", had not been attached to the singular verb "turns out".

YOUR TURN

The New Yorker magazine is a paragon of polished prose, but even it commits the odd howler. Can you spot what went wrong in this sentence?

> *Talk of big European and American banks quitting the City of London, which by many measures is the world's largest financial hub, are exaggerated.*

Answer on page 68

Writing an essay

The most important thing to do in an essay is the most obvious: answer the question. Don't just download everything you know on the subject. There's an old rule that goes, "Say what you're going to say, say it, then say what you've said." It's formulaic, but not a bad tip. The key is to engage the reader from the start, ideally with a brisk, confident sentence. Avoid dull, throat-clearing phrases such as "When considering this question, it is important to..." Get on with your argument, believe in it, and back it up with evidence. If you feel passionate about it, you'll write better (as long as you stay cool enough to read it through at the end). Imagine you're making the case to friends in a coffee shop. How would you persuade them? What would you say to catch their interest? Pretending you are talking to someone also helps you develop an argument that is logical and hangs together.

The last part of that old rule is a good one, too. Sum up what you're saying at the end. Leave your reader in no doubt what you think.

Give reasons for every point you make

The reasons are more important than the point, because they're more likely to be persuasive.

Sound as if you know how you will finish

This was the thing my tutor at Oxford hoped to find in an essay, and as I write, I can still hear him saying it. Think your argument through, and it will show.

Come up with a good line

Good lines don't just come out of nowhere. They come because we work at them. Here are a few to set you thinking.

> Writing free verse is like playing tennis with the net down. **- Robert Frost**

> There is no money in poetry, but then there is no poetry in money, either. **- Robert Graves**

> A lie can be halfway round the world while the truth is putting on its shoes. **- Mark Twain**

25 phrases that are never right

what people say	*what they mean*
Would of, should of, could of	Would have, should have, could have
Each others	Each other's
Over-exaggerate	Exaggerate
The least number of	The fewest
Between you and I	Between you and me
Myself and Kanye	Kanye and I (or me, if it's the object)
Revert back	Revert, or go back
I thought to myself	I said to myself
Up until	Up to, or until
In school	At school
Optimistic of	Hopeful of
Prefer ... over	Prefer ... to
Between ... or	Between ... and

Amount [of a plural]	Number
Less [anything plural]	Fewer
Under the circumstances	In the circumstances (they stand around)
Hone in	Home in (hone means sharpen)
First-year anniversary	First anniversary (anni- means year)
To step foot	To set foot, or to step
One of the only	One of the few
Mens, womens, childrens	Men's, women's, children's
The criteria is	The criteria are The criterion is
Pronounciation	Pronunciation
She was sat on the bench	She sat on the bench
Very unique	Unique (it either is unique or it isn't)

Three words that don't hunt in pairs

An "also" shouldn't be followed by another "also". A "this" shouldn't be followed by another "this" (after "this", go for "that"). A "but" shouldn't be followed by another "but" – it's like asking the reader to do two U-turns in the same street.

Rarely right

I think	It goes without saying.
Utilise	A pretentious word for "use".
Incredible, incredibly	Say something specific, so the reader shares your incredulity.
Hugely	There's no adverb from big or small, much as Donald Trump might want one, because we don't often do things in a big or small way. If you feel the need to beef up an adjective, choose a stronger one.
Just desserts	The perfect phrase for when you come across some fair-minded puddings. If you mean "the result the person deserved", you need "just

	deserts" – an old noun from the same root as "deserved".
The former ... the latter	Sends the reader back: better to use names or pronouns.
Beg the question	"Raise the question" is simpler and better.
Indeed	Handle with care: it may bring a whiff of pomposity.
Focus	Tends to be over-used: try "concentrate".

Never good

Plagiarism	If you want to use someone else's words, just quote them.
Gush	Because writing is cooler and drier than conversation.
Guff	Because each word has to earn its place and pull its weight.
Waffle	Because it's a waste of time.

5. Be organised

When you have a job, you soon realise that half the battle is getting organised. Writing is like that too.

Whether you're writing an essay, a story or a poem, you'll need a beginning, a middle and an end. Whether you have the middle and the end mapped out at the beginning is another matter. "My advice is to write your story first," Philip Pullman told a packed theatre at the Oxford Literary Festival in 2015, "and make the plan afterwards." And he used to be an English teacher.

But you can bet that when he embarked on *His Dark Materials*, he had some inkling of where Lyra and Will would end up, and what would happen to the Authority. It's said that when J.K. Rowling started the first Harry Potter book, she knew how the whole saga would finish, but not how she would get there. A destination is essential, a plan is desirable, and some flexibility is advisable, because you will have more ideas during the writing than you do beforehand. But it's all too easy for advice to be abstract, so here are some practical tips.

Know your priorities

Are you telling a story or making a case? If it's a story, it needs to begin and end with something happening. "The third act must build, build, build in tempo until the last event," the great film-maker Billy Wilder said, "and then ... that's it. Don't hang around."

Hold on to your rabbit

There is always a well-known solution to every
human problem — neat, plausible, and wrong.
                            H.L. Mencken, 1920

At school they taught me how to be
So pure in thought and word and deed.
They didn't quite succeed.
                    Pet Shop Boys, It's a Sin, 1987

Falling Awake   **Alice Oswald, 2016**

Here are three pieces of writing, from different eras,
in different genres – an essay, a song and the title of
a book of poems – and they all obey the same rule:
**the most important word in a sentence is the
last.** Each leads you one way, then surprises you.
None of the sentences is complex, all of the words
are simple, yet each time the effect is satisfying. We
are programmed to enjoy a twist in the tale, and for
maximum impact it should be a twist in the tail, so
the surprise hangs in the air. Alice Oswald pulls her
rabbit out of the hat in the space of two words,
delaying the surprise till the final syllable, playing
off the fact that "asleep" and "awake" begin with the
same sound. Any of us might have noticed that, but
it took a poet to make something of it.

    If the most important word in a sentence is the
last, a few other things follow. Any dull bits need to be
dispatched before the end: if in doubt, park them in

the middle. If a word has come at the end of one sentence, it shouldn't come at the end of the next, or it will have stolen its own thunder. In a list, the final entry should be the strongest one. And in a paragraph, the most important sentence is the last.

Keep your sentences short

The danger with short sentences is that your writing becomes staccato. The danger with long ones is that you lose the plot, and the reader. Which danger is the greater? The second, surely. Ideally, you'll mix up the lengths of your sentences, while leaning to the short side. One of the great long-form stories of recent years was a piece by Michael Pollan for the New York Times Magazine on our messed-up relationship with food. Even though it ran to 10,000 words, it became the most read feature on nytimes. com in 2007, partly on the strength of its opening:

Eat food. Not too much. Mostly plants.

Samuel Beckett had taken the same idea even further in 1969:

Ever tried. Ever failed. No matter. Try again. Fail better.

Contrast those two with this, from a leading economist:

"... the easy presumption of the last two decades of the 20th century that the listed company should not only be the dominant form of economic organisation of medium and large enterprises but the only form of economic organisation appropriate for such enterprises was a mistake. Too often conversion to a listed public company was the result of a greedy generation's anxiety to realise the goodwill created over a long history for the benefit of those who had the good fortune to be around at the time"   **John Kay, FT, 2016**

Try reading that aloud and you'll be gasping for breath. A respected thinker, and a writer with plenty of crisp words in his locker (*easy, greedy, goodwill, fortune*), Kay is so busy thinking here that even the good words end up as croutons, drowning in a goulash of guff.

Hit the return key

Like "and" and "but", paragraphs are your friend. As well as giving the reader a break, they make your thinking clearer and radiate confidence. For some reason, though, this is a card we are often reluctant to play. When writing by hand, we can get sucked into putting down one thing after another, and only realise too late that there was a natural break half way through. When writing on a screen, we can do something about it, so that's the time to get into the habit of making your paragraphs shorter.

As a rule of thumb, **you need a new paragraph for each cluster of thoughts**. If it threatens to get too big, you can split it in two, or three. If you're writing dialogue, you can do what novelists do and start a new paragraph for every new speaker, which makes it a lot clearer who is saying what.

If you're introducing a new point, a new piece of evidence or a new idea, reach for the return key. Do it where it seems logical to give the reader a pause for breath. Try to vary the length of your paragraphs, just as you do with your sentences. Rhythm is almost as important in prose as it is in poetry.

There's a paragraph from a classic comic novel, Evelyn Waugh's *Decline and Fall* (1928), which the publisher of this book, Jon Connell, particularly likes. It shows a Welsh band arriving at a school sports day, as seen by a character called Dr Fagan.

Ten men of revolting appearance were approaching from the drive. They were low of brow, crafty of eye, and crooked of limb. They advanced huddled together with the loping tread of wolves, peering

Answer: Your Turn (page 57)

The main verb should be "is exaggerated", not "are exaggerated", because the subject is "talk".

about them furtively as they came, as though in constant terror of ambush; they slavered at their mouths, which hung loosely over the receding chins, while each clutched under his ape-like arm a burden of curious and unaccountable shape. On seeing the Doctor they halted and edged back, those behind squinting and moulting over their companions' shoulders.

Over to Jon. "A short sentence sets the scene, telling us what happened," he says. "A second short sentence reinforces the first, the sing-song rhythm ('low of brow, crafty of eye') ramming home how ridiculous the musicians seem. Then comes a third, much longer sentence, expanding on the second. The paragraph ends with another shortish sentence which rounds off the picture, telling us what happens when the musicians spot the doctor. (And if you think it's all a bit unfair on Welsh rustics, you're right, but that's comedy for you. Waugh's description of the posh, English Bollinger Club is just as savage.)

"Note how Waugh sticks to the same grammatical subject: the 'ten men of revolting appearance' keep reappearing as 'they'. It's like showing a scene in a film from a single camera angle. It helps us to keep things steady in our minds. In lesser hands the string of *they*s might be too repetitive, but with Waugh's sparkling imagery, varied sentence lengths, and varied word order – making sure that *they* isn't the first word in every sentence – we barely notice."

Beware of the dangler

A sign near a London station advertises the services of a personal trainer. It says: "After sitting on my arse for years, Wayne made me fighting fit again." This is a particularly fine example of a howler known as the dangling participle – the dangler, to its friends.

The word "sitting" in the advert is a participle, a form of a verb that behaves like an adjective, as in "Gone Girl", "Breaking Bad", or "the smoking gun". If a participle, or any other modifier, comes at the start of a sentence, the subject has to be the person to whom it applies. So if you start with "After sitting on my arse for years", the subject can only be "I". Common sense may tell us what the writer of the advert meant, but it's better to mean what you say.

THE SOUL OF WIT

The shortest exchange of letters ever recorded was between the novelist Victor Hugo and his publisher, just after *Les Misérables* came out. Hugo wanted to know how sales were going. He wrote: "?". The sales were excellent. Back came the reply: "!"

Seven bad words

Genuinely has any sentence ever been improved by adding it?

Literally ubiquitous in conversation, perilous on the page

Substantial full of hot air: if a footballer is said to have "substantial technical ability", it just means good technique

Considerable sounds important, means hardly anything

Like, meaning sort of works in conversation, dead on the page

Very indispensable in conversation, but a boomerang on the page – we use it to strengthen our point, only to find that it weakens it

Unsurprisingly (a) clumsy
(b) you might as well say "skip this sentence"

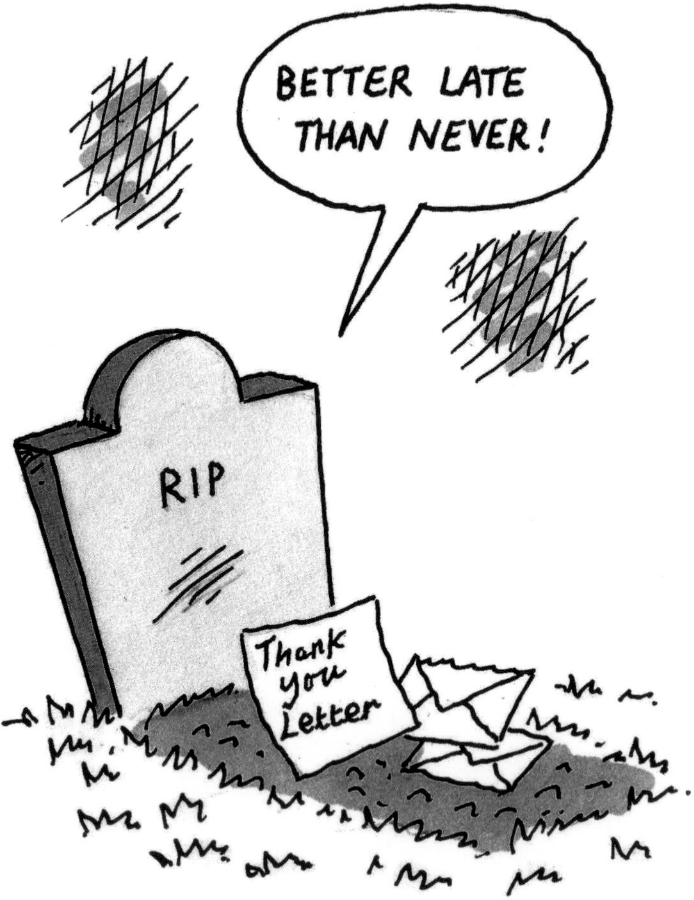
BETTER LATE THAN NEVER!
RIP
Thank you Letter

A BETTER THANK-YOU LETTER

1. Don't see it as a chore. See it as a chance to show your enthusiasm, practise your writing and come up with a memorable line or two.
2. Be specific. Say things you couldn't have said beforehand – not just "thank you for the voucher, it was very generous".
3. Think about what the giver of the present or the party put into it, whether it's the thought or the time spent clearing up afterwards. Broaden out the gratitude if you can, but keep it real: don't gush or perjure yourself.
4. Say something only you can say. Tell the recipient something they don't know – the music you spent the voucher on, the person you had a good chat with at the party, the thing on the menu that was delicious, the song that got you dancing.
5. Don't worry if it's late: this is a clear case of better late than never. Writing a thank-you letter may still not be your idea of fun, but the only alternative is not writing one, which is an easy way to look ungrateful and entitled. But don't go on a guilt trip – we've all done it.

6. Read like a writer

"A reader lives a thousand lives before he dies," said Jojen. "The man who never reads lives only one."
— **George R.R. Martin,** *A Dance with Dragons* **(2011)**

Of all the lines he has written, that is Martin's favourite. It's the story of his own life. "When I was a kid," he said at the Edinburgh International Book Festival in 2014, "my world was five streets long." He lived in a dockside town in New Jersey, the son of a longshoreman. "I never got away, except in books. I lived a thousand lives through books."

Writers need to be open, to words as well as to the rest of the world. They don't just read books, they read newspapers. And they don't choose a newspaper for its politics, because that would be like voting for the candidate who can write the best.

Reading doesn't just broaden the mind: it sharpens the pencil. By writing, you will learn things the hard way; by reading, you can do it the easy way too. You can learn from other people's mistakes, and their successes, and everything in between. **You will see how simple a good line can be.**

"The past is never dead," William Faulkner wrote in *Requiem for a Nun* (1951). "It's not even past."

This was quoted by Barack Obama at a vital moment on his way to the White House in 2008, when he went against the wishes of his advisors and made a speech about race relations. He didn't quite get the quote right, saying "the past is never dead and buried". But it was still Faulkner's line, and the fact that it played a part on the world's biggest stage, 57 years after it was published, triumphantly proved its point.

Writers read in the same ways other people do, for pleasure or escape, to acquire knowledge or to make sense of the human predicament.

> The best moments in reading are when you come across something – a thought, a feeling, a way of looking at things – which you had thought special and particular to you. Now here it is, set down by someone else, a person you have never met, someone even who is long dead. And it is as if a hand has come out and taken yours.
> – **Alan Bennett, *The History Boys* (2006)**

That pleasure is waiting for us whether we write or not. But writers also read in another way, paying close attention. A golfer has to watch the ball, a driver has to watch the road, and **a writer has to watch each word.**

Nobody living in the 21st century needs to know anything about what lovable buffoons, omniscient valets and domineering aunts might have got up to in 1920s England, but P.G. Wodehouse is still read and revered by the writers' union, because they can open a book of his at random and find a sentence like this, from *Very Good, Jeeves* (1930): "In one second, without any previous training or upbringing, he had become the wettest man in Worcestershire."

Writers re-read, sometimes again and again, so that

the plot looms less large and the technique stands out. Writers read with their ears as well as their brains, hearing the lines in their head, letting them ring out, seeing which resound and which fall flat. Writers look and listen hard enough to separate the strengths from the weaknesses, even in authors they admire. There are many reasons to applaud J.K. Rowling: her plotting (seven books of twists and turns), her ingenuity (the sorting hat), her characterisation (Hagrid, Dumbledore, the Weasleys), her powers of realisation (the Dementors), her good humour (Bertie Bott's Every Flavour Beans). But that doesn't mean you have to admire the way she uses adverbs.

> Professor McGonagall sniffed angrily.
>
> "Oh yes, everyone's celebrating, all right," she said impatiently ...
>
> "You can't blame them," said Dumbledore gently. "We've had precious little to celebrate for eleven years."
>
> "I know that," said Professor McGonagall irritably.
>
> **Harry Potter and the Philosopher's Stone (1997)**

Angrily, impatiently, gently, irritably: three of those four could have gone without saying. They are props that are not needed if the dialogue is half-decent, which it is. And they all end up in a prominent place, at the end of their sentence (he added tetchily).

I JUST DON'T WANT TO DISCOURAGE HIM FROM WRITING
POLICE R SCUM
MUFC

7. Write like a writer

In June 2016 the people of Britain astonished themselves by voting to leave the European Union. A week later, the Financial Times had two columnists writing about how this fateful moment had gone for them. Here's a paragraph from each.

> I was quite confident during the day that Remain would win, reinforced by the late opinion polls. However, results from Newcastle and Sunderland sharply changed my mood as I departed for bed, and by 6am it was all over – Brexit had triumphed.
>
> – **John Lee**

> All good dramas involve the suspension of disbelief. So it was with Brexit. I went to bed at 4am on Friday depressed that Britain had voted to leave the EU. The following day my gloom only deepened. But then, belatedly, I realised that I have seen this film before. I know how it ends. And it does not end with the UK leaving Europe.
>
> – **Gideon Rachman**

The two paragraphs have plenty in common: both mention bed, both pinpoint a time of day, both express disappointment, both use the first person freely. But only one reads like the work of a writer.

In John Lee's paragraph, something goes mildly amiss in every line. When he says "quite confident", it's not clear if he is using "quite" in the British sense (fairly) or the American (wholly). When he tacks on "reinforced" at the end of a clause in which the subject was "I", he is saying that he, not his confidence, was reinforced by the polls, which isn't the way "reinforce" works; he'd be better off with "fortified".

He then reaches for "however", which, as so often, is clunky and unnatural – a sledgehammer being used to crack a "but". My guess is that he wanted to say "but", only to hear the voice of a long-dead schoolteacher in his head, saying you shouldn't begin a sentence with a conjunction. Which is nonsense.

And what did the referendum results do to his mood? They "sharply changed" it. **This isn't writing, it's Russian athletics coaching: an attempt to take an ordinary verb and put it on steroids.** The attempt backfires because the wording still feels weak. If you want to strengthen a verb, replace it with a stronger one. The thesaurus has plenty to offer: "transform", "darken", "sour", "ruin".

Worst of all, the paragraph finishes by saying that Brexit had triumphed, thereby telling FT readers something they already knew. There is a place for things the reader knows, but that place is not the end of a paragraph. It turns a dive into a belly flop.

Rachman's way of saying much the same thing is sharper. He opens with a big pronouncement: "All good dramas involve the suspension of disbelief." It's a generalisation, and thus a gamble – if the reader can think of a single exception, Rachman will have put some of his own credibility in the toaster. But he gets away with it, partly because he moves on so fast.

It's not the only thing he gets away with. In the middle of his paragraph are two or three bum notes. "Depressed" isn't quite the right word for how he felt, as it suggests a mood that is prolonged; he might have been better off with "dismayed", "disheartened" or "downcast". (When he returns to his mood, he makes a better choice – "gloom".) He too places the result at the end of a sentence. He picks up on "4am on Friday" with "the following day", which is a bit jarring (once you've gone specific, stay specific) and confusing: does he mean later on Friday, or Saturday? But his rhythm is impeccable, with its short brisk sentences, and it carries us along to the part of the paragraph that matters most – the end.

He's been talking about drama, and he has a twist of his own: Brexit is not going to happen after all. It's a rabbit produced from a hat, the opposite of Lee's floppy ending. It is proper writing. Not to dismiss Lee, whose column exists to give investment advice; for him, the advice is more important than the wording. Rachman, one of the FT's big guns, needs to write like a writer – and does.

Here are a few more leaves you can take out of the professionals' book.

Be curious

Ask questions, or just listen. Some writers are good talkers, but more of them are good listeners. For non-fiction, they need information and ideas; for fiction, ideas and feelings, and sometimes information too; for both, a feel for human nature.

To write, you will need to have things to say. **To have things to say, you will need to listen,** to absorb, to learn from people who have seen and done interesting things. If you're stuck next to an older person, you could ask what life was like for them at your age. Something they say will surprise you.

Just write ...

It doesn't have to be for publication – better not, to begin with. You could keep a diary, not daily, not religiously, but every now and again. **Write the way you take photographs**, to capture something striking. Write the way you talk about your feelings, to release something. Or not: it doesn't have to be your innermost thoughts – you could be the kind of writer who looks outwards and slips more easily into the third person than the first. If a diary seems too daunting, just take notes on a journey, a project, a new stage of life. One way or another, get into the habit of putting some words down.

... And rewrite

Write something, leave it to cool, come back a few days later. It will strike you differently; you may well see things to improve. It may be in need of a polish, a trim, a full rethink, or nothing at all. **Half of writing is rewriting.** Unlike in conversation, you are free to get it wrong first time, and even the best writers need that freedom. There was once a spin bowler who was so slow, it was said that if he didn't like the ball he had just bowled, he could go and fetch it before it reached the batsman. When we write, we are all that bowler.

Don't write with just your brain

Write with your eyes, your ears, your heart – more of those things if it's fiction, more brain if it's something analytical. But make sure the heart still plays a part.

Develop a voice

You already have a voice in the literal sense (the ability to talk) and you probably have one in the literary sense too (a distinctive way with a phrase). But the first thing to do here, as so often, is to **steer away from the rocks of self-consciousness.**

It's easier to make out someone else's voice than your own. Picture a friend or member of your family talking to you: what are their favourite words, their characteristic tone, the rhythms of their speech? These are the ingredients that make a voice.

Before we're even aware of it, we have a distinctive voice – in fact two, one for writing and one for speaking. The two are siblings, perhaps even twins, but not identical. When writing, we make certain adjustments – no ums and ers, no swearing (unless it's strictly necessary, which probably means you're writing dialogue or quoting), a wider vocabulary, some longer sentences. But we shouldn't take this too far. Some of the worst writing turns up when the writer believes that writing is a different language, and starts replacing good, clear, direct words with stilted ones – "begin" becomes "commence", "also" becomes "in addition", "a lot" becomes "a substantial amount", "shown" becomes "evidenced", and the reader smells waffle or, worse, bullshit.

All this may take years. Paul Greengrass, the director of the best of the Bourne films, started out as a documentary maker and was nearly 50 before he made an action movie. He soon became revered for his distinctive style – relentless drama, hand-held cameras, a hotline to the viewer's nervous system. Now, when he talks to film students, he says this:

Find the song that only you can sing.

Be original

Originality sounds like a high bar to jump over, but it begins with a single thought.

You put together two things that have not been put together before. And the world is changed... –
– **Julian Barnes**, *Levels of Life* (2013)

Put different flavours together

As you get older, bitter chocolate is better chocolate. And so it is with writing: hundreds of great love songs are bittersweet. Here's Tom Stoppard being entertaining and erudite at the same time, and liking the effect so much that he uses it to open a play:

> *Precocious teenager, about 200 years ago, to her tutor:*
> Septimus, what is carnal embrace?
> *Tutor, suddenly spotting her mother:*
> It is the practice of throwing one's arms around a
> side of beef.   ***Arcadia* (1993)**

Express yourself, not someone else

"I am trying to express my way of being in the world. This is primarily a process of elimination: once you have removed all the dead language, the second-hand dogma, the truths that are not your own but other people's, the mottos, the slogans, the out-and-out lies of your nation, the myths of your historical moment – once you have removed all that warps experience into a shape you do not recognise and do not believe in – what you are left with is something approximating the truth of your own conception."
                    – **Zadie Smith, *Fail Better* (2007)**

Don't wait for inspiration

It does exist – sometimes a fresh idea will pop into your head, apparently unprompted. But **inspiration seldom has more than a cameo role**. The lead goes to something more earthbound: concentration, application, grit. And that you can control.

Don't fall for the first word you meet

"Brilliant" is another word that is becoming too weary to do its job. It's supposed to mean "shining brightly", but is now trotted out so often, in British English at least, that it has come to mean just "very good". If that's what you mean, you're better off with "outstanding"; if you want to keep the element of sheen, try "sparkling" or "scintillating". Or turn to the thesaurus: this is what it's for.

Keep it up your sleeve

Readers love **a bit of suspense**. "Narrative tension," the novelist Ian McEwan has said, "is primarily about withholding information." It's a rather grey line by his high standards, but a true one.

Jane Eyre begins like this: "There was no possibility of taking a walk that day." And instantly you want to know why. Before introducing a character, Charlotte Brontë has drawn you into her web.

Be subtle

Life is full of fine distinctions, so writing needs to be subtle. But subtle can still be simple. "I don't believe in God," Julian Barnes once said, "but I miss him."

Mind your metaphors and similes

A simile and a metaphor are a pair of sisters, both bright, one bolder than the other. A simile usually involves a *like* or an *as*, whereas a metaphor declares firmly that X is Y. Here are six for the price of one:

> A library in the middle of a community is a cross between an emergency exit, a life-raft and a festival. They are cathedrals of the mind; hospitals of the soul; theme parks of the imagination. On a cold rainy island, they are the only sheltered public spaces where you are not a consumer, but a citizen.
> **Caitlin Moran, Moranthology** (2013)

Moran didn't really need those semi-colons, and six metaphors on one plate may be too much for some tastes. But they are good ones, powered by passion.

The point isn't just to liken X to Y. It's to liken X to a Y that is **part of the reader's world**. Homer compares an army to a field of corn, because every last member of his audience would have known what that field looked like. It's the same when Shakespeare compares a lover to a summer's day.

Some are old friends, and that's fine ...

There are metaphors that people reach for all the time: *not my cup of tea, barking up the wrong tree, plenty of fish in the sea, needle in a haystack, water under the bridge, another string to her bow*. Orwell thought we should avoid them (like the plague). He was being too hard-line: these phrases have become part of the furniture because they're useful.

There are some words that now exist largely, or even only, in metaphors – hoist by your own petard, damp squib, poisoned chalice. That's OK too: it adds colour and texture to everyday life.

... But if they're too old, play with them

One man's meat is another man's – the standard word is poison, but by now we know where you're going and you can replace it with almost anything.

Keep your metaphors metaphorical ...

Some metaphors become drained of their ability to take us into a different field. "The lies of Britain's papers have been key to shaping the country's predicament," says Open Democracy. But keys don't shape anything. They're for opening doors. One way to remind yourself of this is to say "a key" rather than just "key". A key is not an adjective.

... And try not to mix them

A footballer with a rare talent: hugging pictures.

The thing that sets Steph Houghton apart from the
rest, the quality that has made her the captain of
Manchester City and England, is an ability to
embrace the bigger picture.

The Observer, April 2016

There's nothing like a simile

Writers see parallels in unexpected places.

Like a bird on the wire
Like a drunk in a midnight choir
I have tried, in my way, to be free

Leonard Cohen, *Bird on the Wire* (1969)

**If you're making a fresh simile, as Cohen was, you
may need the "like". But it is never essential:**

War is capitalism with the gloves off.

Tom Stoppard, *Travesties* (1974)

Find the paradox

Writers look at things sideways. Or upside down:

The child is father of the man.

William Wordsworth,
My Heart Leaps Up When I Behold **(1802)**

Miss Brooke had that kind of beauty which seems
to be thrown into relief by poor dress.

George Eliot, opening *Middlemarch* **(1871-72)**

And I call to you, I call to you,
But I don't call soft enough.

Leonard Cohen, *Ain't No Cure for Love* **(1988)**

YOUR TURN

1. Which of these are metaphors?

a) All the world's a stage.
— Shakespeare, *As You Like It*

b) I became aware of someone coughing softly by my side, like a respectful sheep trying to catch the attention of its shepherd.
— P.G. Wodehouse, *Thank You, Jeeves*

c) In Raymond Chandler's The Big Sleep, *the hero notices that the trees at a grand house were "trimmed as carefully as poodle dogs".*

d) Jeeves lugged my purple socks out of the drawer as if he were a vegetarian fishing a caterpillar out of his salad. **— Wodehouse, *My Man Jeeves***

Answers on page 94

2. Write a paragraph about a city you know, using only natural imagery.

3. "If phrases are old friends, play around with them." Here are three more sentences from Wodehouse and one by Garrison Keillor, all of which do this.

The supply of the milk of human kindness was short by several gallons.

Hell, it is well known, has no fury like a woman who wants her tea and can't get it.

I'd always thought her half-baked, but now I think they didn't even put her in the oven.

She hasn't just got a screw loose – the whole lid's blown off.

a) Give these phrases a twist so they don't feel stale.

You could have knocked me down with a feather.

It was the best thing since sliced bread.

b) Finish these sentences in the style of Wodehouse.

He was as angry as ...

She sprang out of bed like ...

4. Finish this line in the spirit of Julian Barnes (page 86)

I don't believe in private education, but...

Having fun with Free Indirect Speech

Emma, in the novel of the same name (1815), is as clever and witty as any of Jane Austen's heroines. But she is also spoilt and obsessed with status. To take us inside her head, Austen uses a trick she became famous for: the technique known as Free Indirect Speech. Here is the moment when Emma meets a girl from the local school, Harriet Smith.

> She was not struck by any thing remarkably clever in Miss Smith's conversation, but she found her altogether very engaging – not inconveniently shy, not unwilling to talk – and yet so far from pushing, shewing so proper and becoming a deference, seeming so pleasantly grateful for being admitted to Hartfield, and so artlessly impressed by the appearance of every thing in so superior a style to what she had been used to, that she must have good sense and deserve encouragement. Encouragement should be given. Those soft blue eyes and all those natural graces should not be wasted on the inferior society of Highbury and its connections.

These are Emma's thoughts, yet Austen never says "she thought". The narrator is telling the story, but what we are hearing are Emma's judgements of Harriet in Emma's words ("not inconveniently shy ... so far from pushing ... so artlessly impressed"). In showing us these judgements, or shewing them as she would say, Austen is also showing how vain and egotistical her heroine is – how she loves to have people defer to her; how her concern is her own convenience, not Harriet's; how what she really likes is the way Harriet recognises her as her superior. She persuades herself that she's going to be nice to Harriet because it will be good for Harriet, when it is really because she is bored and wants someone to play with. So the reader can relish Austen's voice (all those commas) at the same time as grasping what it feels like to be Emma.

Answer: Your Turn (page 90)

All are similes except the first, which is a metaphor.

Store the bad stuff

You don't have to suffer for your art, but it can help. Anything that goes wrong in life can be stashed away to be used as fuel for your writing. Social awkwardness? Personal turmoil? Trouble with bullies? Sorry to hear it, but it's all good material.

Revise the received wisdom

Sometimes the received wisdom is wise enough. But what if it doesn't ring true? As soon as you query it or vary it, you have some wisdom of your own.

> The greatest lie ever told about love is that it sets you free. **Zadie Smith, *On Beauty* (2005)**

Make it sing

Work on your sentence till it has some music to it. Make it sing, make it dance – and feel the benefit. When this works, it won't just be the sentence that gets better. **You will have found something in yourself that you didn't know was there.**

We need to talk about ... writer's block

Every writer, professional or otherwise, knows how it feels to find the words refusing to flow. Here's one way of getting round it.

1. **Resist the urge to panic.**

2. Ask yourself what has to be in there, however simple.

3. Start making a list of these things.

4. As you make it, think about what order the things should go in and move them up or down the list.

5. Congratulate yourself – you've started writing.

8. A few good models

That's enough advice: let's have a quick look at some top-class writing, all of it modern.

How to start an epic

The Decanter of Tokay

Lyra and her daemon moved through the darkening Hall, taking care to keep to one side, out of sight of the kitchen. The three great tables that ran the length of the Hall were laid already, the silver and the glass catching what little light there was, and the long benches were pulled out ready for the guests. Portraits of former Masters hung high up in the gloom along the walls. Lyra reached the dais and looked back at the open kitchen door and, seeing no one, stepped up beside the high table. The places here were laid with gold, not silver, and the fourteen seats were not oak benches but mahogany chairs with velvet cushions.

Lyra stopped beside the Master's chair and flicked the biggest glass gently with a fingernail. The sound rang clearly through the Hall.

"You're not taking this seriously," whispered her daemon. "Behave yourself."

Her daemon's name was Pantalaimon, and he was currently in the form of a moth, a dark brown one so as not to show up in the darkness of the Hall.

"They're making too much noise to hear from the kitchen," Lyra whispered back. "And the Steward doesn't come in till the first bell. Stop fussing."
Northern Lights, 1995

Philip Pullman shows us that his heroine is fearless – and so is he. He heads his first chapter *The Decanter of Tokay*, happy to use not one word that may well be new to his young readers, but two. He plunges us *in medias res*, as the Romans said– into the thick of things – and his first four words pick up on Rome's greatest poem. "Arms and the man" is the way Virgil opens *The Aeneid*. "Lyra and her daemon" is an echo, a homage, and an incentive to read on: what's a daemon? Again, Pullman doesn't explain. He just shows us the scene, the sights and sounds of the Hall. His vocab is brisk and vivid: in the first paragraph, the only words longer than two syllables are *darkening* and *mahogany*. He laces his sentences with alliteration: *length, laid, little light, long; hung high; flicked, fingernail.* He doesn't fret about repetition, putting two *not*s in one sentence, and two *with*s with them, and using "whispered" twice, when many writers would have opted for an inelegant variation. He keeps showing us the shortage of light (*darkening, gloom, dark brown, darkness*) and the texture of things (*silver, glass, gold, oak, mahogany, velvet*). His dark materials.

He sketches the relationship between Lyra and Pantalaimon, letting them talk like a brother and sister (*Behave yourself, Stop fussing*). Even before we turn a page, we know that their exchanges will show Lyra's innermost feelings. And although this is a fantasy trilogy, in which many weird and wonderful things will happen, the only fantastical element in the first scene is Pan. He is given a gender, but no further explanation – just a single word, "currently", to let slip that he is a shape-shifter. Daemons are the most memorable of Pullman's creations, and he has enough confidence in them to want us to get to know them bit by bit. It's the sort of decision-making that can keep you enthralled for 1200 pages.

How to capture a stage of life

Remember the time
When everyone was like a seal
Before the wax hardened.
Each of us bears the stamp
Of a friend met along the way –
In everyone, the trace of everyone.
For better or worse,
For wiser or sillier,
Everyone imprinted with everyone.
Primo Levi, part of *To My Friends*, 1985, published in *The Mirror Maker*, 1990; original in Italian, translation my own

There's an English word, impressionable, which often appears in a single phrase – an impressionable age, covering all the stages we go through from toddler to adult. This poem takes that idea and runs with it, capturing the impact of our early friendships.

Primo Levi keeps it beautifully simple, saying "everyone" again and again and using the same metaphor in three or four guises (*seal, stamp, trace, imprinted*). By concentrating, he hits the nail on the head. Levi had seen humanity at its most inhuman: the writing he is best known for is his testimony from Auschwitz. But here he looks back, beyond that, to a happier and more normal experience.

Poetry tends to pop up when it is most needed. I wouldn't know this poem if I hadn't lost my brother, Charlie, who died of a sudden illness in 2014, at the age of 54. We asked a couple of his old friends to read something at his memorial service, and one of them went for this. It was an inspired choice, direct, memorable and piercingly true.

Charlie was two years older than me, so I followed him to school and university, and when he found a new enthusiasm, I tended to catch it like a bug. Sitting in the front pew listening to the poem, I thought about all the imprints he had left on me. In the words of Alan Bennett (page 75), it was as if a hand had come out of a book and taken mine, which, at that moment, needed holding.

Primo Levi's words made a deep impression on a lot of people that day. And they highlighted the one problem with the way we talk about there being an impressionable age: it never really ends. The wax doesn't have to harden.

How to have fun with a classic form

The Economist, a weekly news magazine, is famous for not telling its readers the names of its writers. But there is one person on the staff whose work is easily spotted. Every week, after spending 60 pages telling us the world's problems can be solved with looser trade regulations, The Economist gives us a treat: an obituary. It's the most soulful thing in the whole magazine. The author is nearly always Ann Wroe, a biographer with a gift for getting inside the head of her subject. Obituaries have hardly anything to do with death: they're all about capturing a life. On this occasion, it wasn't the life of a person.

Peterborough, in the English Midlands, is a red-brick town, best known as the midway point on the line between King's Cross and York. But from the bottom of Kingfisher Lake, just outside it, urban toil seems far away. There, all is most delightful silt and slime. A push of your probing nose sends up puffs and clouds of fine mud through the water. A riff of bubbles rises, silvery, towards the surface. The green reeds quiver, and sunlight ripples down almost to the depths where you are lurking, plump and still.

Such was mostly the life, and such was the address, of Benson, England's most famous fish. Her actual place of birth, as a wriggling, transparent fry prey to every frog, pike and heron, was never known. But at ten, when she was stocked in Kingfisher, she was already a bruiser. And there, among the willow-

shaded banks, she grew. And grew. At her peak
weight, in 2006, she was 64lb 2oz (29kg), and was
almost circular, like a puffed-up plaice. Bigger carp
have been seen in Thailand and in France; but she
still amounted to a lot of gefilte fish.

In her glory days she reminded some of Marilyn
Monroe, others of Raquel Welch. She was lither
than either as she cruised through the water-weed, a
lazy twist of gold.

The Economist, 13 August 2009

The piece gets off to a slow start: if I'd been Ann's editor, I would have politely suggested that Peterborough was a red herring. But as soon as you reach "silt and slime", **you hear a voice ring out.** And with "a push of your probing nose", we find that not only is the writer putting herself in the position of another species, but she's putting us there too. Like Philip Pullman, Ann Wroe uses short vivid words and staggered alliteration (*silt, slime; push, probing, puffs; silvery, surface; reeds, ripples*). With "a riff of bubbles", she mints a phrase, and it's a beauty, turning a sight into a sound, recasting something silent as a sequence of notes.

Ann has dropped us in the water, but she still hasn't introduced her subject. Now she does, making sure to put "Benson, England's most famous fish" at the end of its sentence. She shows us Benson as a baby, in a flash of Disney-ish pathos, then, more brusquely, as "a bruiser". She has some fun with Benson's dimensions, and doesn't flinch from the fact that, for humans, carp is usually a meal. She has more fun with the celebrities to whom Benson was compared: two Hollywood goddesses dating from the curvaceous era.

Reading that sentence, I wondered why Ann had bothered with Raquel Welch, who doesn't add much to the more celebrated Marilyn Monroe. The reason becomes clear a moment later, with "she was lither than either". All the fun has been building up to this line, which takes a familiar adjective, "lithe", and carries it into the uncharted waters of the comparative, just so that it can rhyme with "either". The pleasure Ann is taking in her work has become contagious. But she is not just playing it for laughs: by the end of the sentence, she has changed gear again, going for poetry in "a lazy twist of gold".

How to make a modern fable

Once upon a time, a hundred years ago, there was a dark and stormy girl.

The girl was Russian, and although her hair and eyes and fingernails were dark all of the time, she was stormy only when she thought it absolutely necessary. Which was fairly often.

Her name was Feodora.

She lived in a wooden house made of timber taken from the surrounding forest. The walls were layered with sheep's wool to keep out the Russian winter, and the inside was lit with hurricane lamps.

Feo had painted the lamps every colour in her box of paints, so the house cast out light into the forest in reds and greens and yellows. Her mother had cut and sanded the door herself, and the wood was eight inches thick. Feo had painted it snow blue. The wolves had added claw marks over the years, which helped dissuade unwelcome visitors.

It all began – all of it – with someone knocking on the snow-blue door.

Although 'knocking' was not the right word for this particular noise, Feo thought. It sounded as though someone was trying to dig a hole in the wood with his knuckles.

But any knocking at all was unusual. Nobody knocked: it was just her and her mother and the wolves. Wolves do not knock. If they want to come in, they come in through the window, whether it is open or not.

Katherine Rundell, *The Wolf Wilder* (2015)

Anyone born since the mid-1980s has lived through a golden age of children's literature. When Kate Rundell (b. 1987) was growing up in Zimbabwe, a parcel arrived for her 11th birthday: the first book about a boy she'd never heard of, Harry Potter. Diving into it, she found that Harry was a month older than her. "I fell in love with him," she wrote later, "or if not with him, because he is the least sharply drawn character, then with the secret world lying so discreetly alongside my own." When she grew up, she became a Fellow of All Souls, the

Oxford college that is so clever, it doesn't have any students, just dons. She became an expert on John Donne, a very grown-up poet. But she hasn't lost her love of children's stories and now she writes them herself. This is the opening page of her third novel.

When you write for children, you have to work out what you can trust the reader to handle. Rundell finds a subtle answer to this question, mixing classic simplicity with modern sophistication. Her language is like a mountain stream, bright and clear and flowing. The first seven verbs in her story are *was, was, were, was, thought, was* and *was*. The opening words are the oldest gambit in town, *once upon a time*. But there's a twist, in fact two: rather than using those words to express timelessness, Rundell pitches her tent in a particular period, whose significance becomes clear when she adds a location. Then she plays off another familiar phrase with *a dark and stormy girl*. In the space of one line, she has set out two stalls, suggesting that her tale will be a fable, and also a laugh. The second paragraph, after briskly introducing us to her heroine, ends on the same note of knowing humour.

The third paragraph is only four words long, which tells us that (a) Feodora is important, and (b) Rundell agrees with Orwell, who advocated varying paragraph length for maximum effect. The fourth paragraph is a scene-setter, a feast for the senses made up of texture (the wood, the wool) and colour (the lamps, the paints), including a shade that is deliciously fresh – not snow-white, but snow-blue.

The fourth paragraph also introduces Feo's house-mates, in two sentences that are models of show and tell. The sentence about the door is quietly feminist, showing that Feo's mother has no need of a man about the house. The sentence about the wolves gets a lot of mileage out of one of the plainest words in the language: *the*. Rundell drops in "the wolves" the way you or I might say "the dogs", which tells us the wolves are part of the household.

Soon she is using the first word in the book that might puzzle an eight-year-old: "dissuade". She is prepared to risk trusting her young readers a little too much, which is the right side to err on. "They can always guess," she said when quizzed about this at the Story Museum in Oxford. "Or ask a grown-up."

The fifth paragraph is another intensely short one. It gives us what is known in Hollywood – where this story may well end up – as the inciting incident: the event that sets the plot in motion.

At the museum, Rundell read some extracts from her book, and one ended as this one does, with the wolves' policy on windows, which got a laugh. Sitting at the back, I witnessed another strength of her sentences: they are easy to read aloud. Although she still has a soft spot for J.K. Rowling, Rundell belongs to the Pullman school of storytelling. Feo is a heroine like Lyra, fearless and resourceful. Her world mixes elements of the real and the fantastical, and the prose rattles along, delivering sophisticated suspense. *The Wolf Wilder* earns the quote that appears on its cover: *'A triumph' – Philip Pullman*.

Afterword

This book was dreamed up by Jon Connell, an editor who is also an inventor – of the Connell Guides and The Week magazine. Many thanks to him for trusting me with it, and to Samantha Weinberg for bringing us together. Thanks also to Nick Newman for his lovable cartoons; to Paul Woodward for his cool-headed production skills; to Jonny Patrick, Shivaun Mason and Malcolm Hebron for setting my compass; to Joe Hartley for suggesting Your Turn; to Araminta Whitley for her wise guidance; to countless colleagues for putting up with my pedantry; to Amanda, Dan and Laura for living with it; and to you, for reading.

A few final suggestions, so short that you can take a picture of them on your phone:

Keep a diary
(as irregular as you like, and private to start with)
Pick up a paper
(wouldn't it be great if someone with a good eye gave you the best stories of the day? Oh, they already do)
Learn a language
(it will sharpen your English)
Join a library
("every book you find has friends it wants to introduce you to, like a party in the library that need never end" – Caitlin Moran)
Start a magazine
(every school should have one, if only a sheet of A4)

Index

of authors and **main topics**

ℂG CONNELL GUIDES

Concise, intelligent guides to history and literature

CONNELL GUIDES TO LITERATURE

Novels and poetry
Emma
Far From the Madding Crowd
Frankenstein
Great Expectations
Hard Times
Heart of Darkness
Jane Eyre
Lord of the Flies
Mansfield Park
Middlemarch
Mrs Dalloway
Paradise Lost
Persuasion
Pride and Prejudice
Tess of the D'Urbervilles
The Canterbury Tales
The Great Gatsby
The Poetry of Robert Browning
The Waste Land
To Kill A Mockingbird
Wuthering Heights

Shakespeare
A Midsummer Night's Dream
Antony and Cleopatra
Hamlet
Julius Caesar

King Lear
Macbeth
Othello
Romeo and Juliet
The Second Tetralogy
The Tempest
Twelfth Night

Modern texts
A Doll's House
A Room with a View
A Streetcar Named Desire
An Inspector Calls
Animal Farm
Atonement
Beloved
Birdsong
Hullabaloo
Never Let Me Go
Of Mice and Men
Rebecca
Spies
The Bloody Chamber
The Catcher in the Rye
The History Boys
The Road
Vernon God Little
Waiting for Godot